Slow Changes on Earth

Nicolas Brasch

Contents

Earth Is Changing

Did you know that Earth's surface is constantly changing? It changes in many different ways and is changed by many different things.

Some changes on Earth have happened because the land on Earth moves. Other changes are caused by wind, water, and ice. Many of these changes have happened very slowly.

The Moving Continents

Earth has seven large areas of land called **continents**. Africa, for example, is a continent. But these areas of land weren't always separate. Millions of years ago, they were joined together in one huge continent.

The continents separated slowly, over millions of years. These drawings show how the world might have looked at different times up to the present.

From One to Seven

How did one continent change into seven? This change happened very slowly. Over millions of years, the one huge continent split into smaller **land masses**. Then these land masses slowly moved apart.

Even today, the continents on Earth are moving very slowly. Millions of years from now, Earth may look very different from the way it looks today!

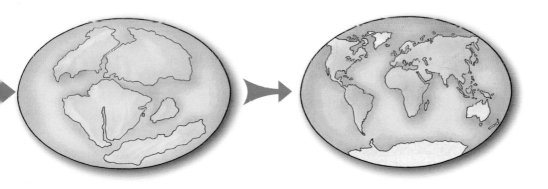

Putting the Pieces Together

How do we know that all the land on Earth was once one big continent?

The shape of the continents gives us one clue. If you look at a map of Earth, you will see that continents in different parts of the world could almost fit together like a jigsaw puzzle. For example, the east coast of South America would fit into the west coast of Africa. Scientists believe that they were once joined.

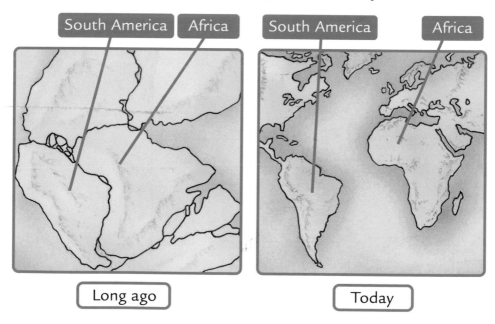

South America   Africa

Long ago

South America   Africa

Today

Scientists have also discovered the same kinds of plants and animals on different continents. For example, there is a bird called a rhea that lives in South America. Rheas cannot fly and are a lot like ostriches, which live in Africa. Scientists believe that both birds come from the same family and were separated when the continents split apart.

Rheas live in South America.

Ostriches live in Africa.

Earth on a Plate

By now, you're probably wondering how a continent can move. The land you're standing on doesn't usually look like it's moving. It took a long time for scientists to find out how large masses of land move.

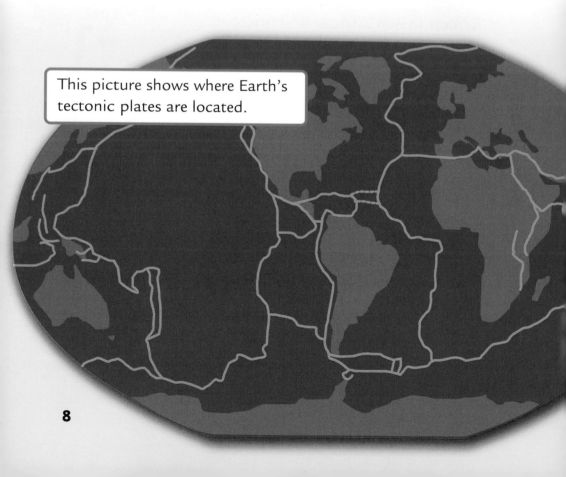

This picture shows where Earth's tectonic plates are located.

Scientists discovered that all the land on Earth sits on huge pieces of rock called **tectonic plates**. These plates form Earth's crust. Even the land under the oceans sits on these plates.

Underneath Earth's crust is a layer of hot, melted rock called magma. The tectonic plates move very slowly on top of this melted rock.

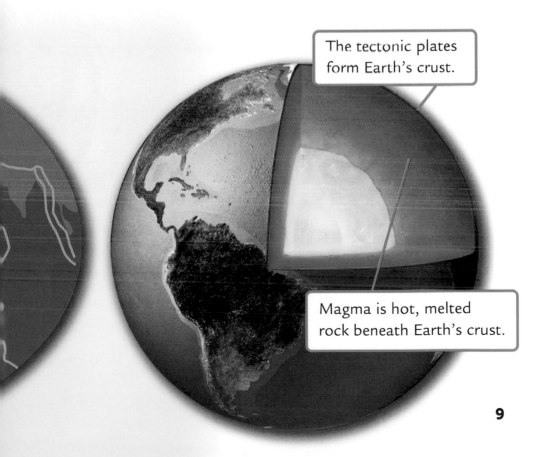

The tectonic plates form Earth's crust.

Magma is hot, melted rock beneath Earth's crust.

The Power of Ice

Earth's continents have changed in other ways, too. Today, only about one-tenth of Earth's surface is covered by ice. Most of this ice is in the areas around the North Pole and the South Pole.

But in the past, there have been times when much more of Earth's surface was covered by ice. These times are known as ice ages.

Ice Ages

Scientists believe that the most recent ice age lasted about a hundred thousand years. It ended about ten thousand years ago. During this ice age, all of Canada was covered in ice. Some parts of Canada were covered by ice more than two miles thick!

This picture shows what North America looked like 15,000 years ago.

Canada

United States of America

11

Moving Ice

Ice doesn't only sit on top of the Earth. Sometimes, it moves across the land, changing Earth's surface.

High in the mountains, the temperature is so cold that snow and ice do not melt. Over many years, more and more snow builds up.

Sometimes, the layers of snow and ice start to slide across each other. These huge, moving sheets of ice and snow are called glaciers.

As a glacier slides across the land, soil and rocks get caught in the bottom layers of ice. The glacier gradually carries away more and more soil, and a valley is formed.

These mountains and valleys were shaped by glaciers.

Glaciers can also break large rocks. Sometimes melted ice flows into a crack in the rock. When the ice freezes again, it expands. This makes the crack bigger. Eventually, a piece of rock snaps off and is carried away in the glacier.

In time, glaciers can travel far from the place where they started. Sometimes they travel to places where the temperature is warmer. As the glacier begins to melt, the rocks and soil that have been caught in the ice are left in new places. Sometimes, huge rocks can be left hundreds of miles from where the glacier picked them up.

This rock was broken off and carried along by a glacier. When the glacier melts, the rock will be left in a new place.

Wind

Wind can change Earth's surface. It can also change the shape of the land.

Near the Sea

Have you ever been to the sea? Have you felt the wind that blows across the beach? Over time, this wind can form hills of sand called sand dunes.

Sometimes plants grow on the sides of sand dunes near the beach. These plants help stop the sand from blowing away. The sand dunes can become an environment where plants and animals can live.

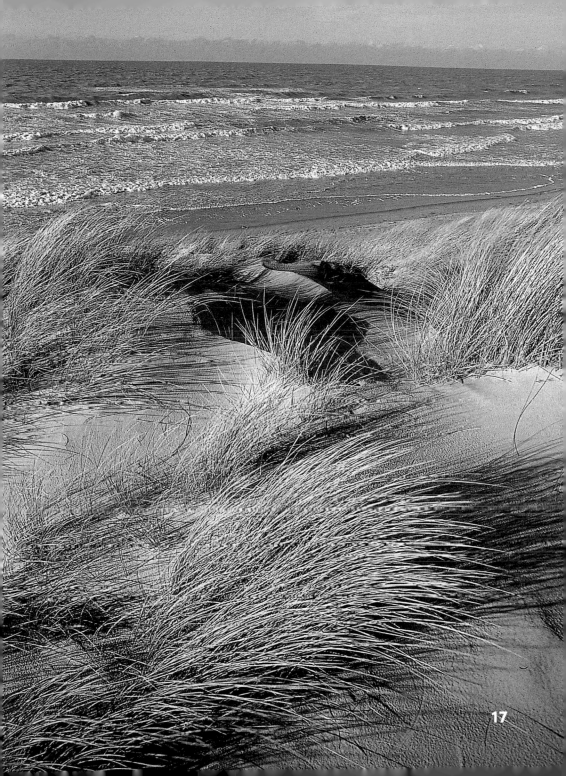

In the Desert

Wind makes sand dunes in the **desert**, too. These sand dunes are changing the shape of the land all the time.

Sand dunes form when the wind blows a lot of sand to one area. Some sand dunes can be more than 1,600 feet tall. That's taller than ten Statues of Liberty on top of each other!

You might think that sand dunes are like normal hills that stay in one place. But they're not. Sand dunes can actually move across the desert.

When a sand dune becomes very tall, the sand at the top slides down the back of the dune. This sand forms a new dune behind the old one. The wind keeps blowing sand off the first dune to form new dunes. Eventually these new dunes move in the direction of the wind.

The wind can change the land near deserts, too. Over thousands of years, wind can blow so much sand over the land that the **landscape** changes completely.

Water

You already know that ice can change the surface of Earth. And ice is just water that has frozen. But did you know that water doesn't have to freeze to change Earth? Water can change **coastlines** and plains. It can even change Earth underground!

Sometimes parts of a coastline are worn away more quickly than the rest. When this happens, large stacks of rock are left standing in the sea.

Cliffs

The coastline of every continent is always changing. Waves crash against cliffs, washing away tiny pieces of rock and sand. The cliffs begin to change shape, but the changes usually happen so slowly that we don't see them happening.

Canyons and Gullies

Water can make **canyons** and **gullies**, too.
Fast-moving streams and rivers wash away the
soil and rock around them. Gradually, as more
and more soil is carried away, a river can
create a deep ditch or valley with steep sides.

Sometimes this process can continue for
millions of years. This is how the Grand
Canyon in the United States was formed.

Caves

Some **caves** are formed by rainwater that soaks into the surface of the Earth.

As rain falls, the rainwater mixes with carbon dioxide, a gas that is found in air and soil. Together, water and carbon dioxide can **erode** some kinds of rock.

As the rock is eroded, a cave is slowly formed under the ground. This process can take thousands of years.

Glossary

canyon   a deep valley with steep sides

cave   an opening under the ground

coastline   the outline of the land where it meets the sea

continent   one of the main land masses on Earth

desert   a sandy or rocky place where there is little or no rain

erode   to wear away

gully   a small valley worn away by water

land mass   a large piece of land surrounded by ocean

landscape   the natural shape of Earth's surface

tectonic plate   a huge section of Earth's crust